MW01040942

Animal show and tell

Animals in the Desert

Élisabeth de Lambilly-Bresson

Gareth Stevens
Publishing

The Fennec Fox

I am a fennec fox.
In the fox family,
I am the smallest,
but I have the biggest ears.
I love to lie around
in the desert Sun.
Some people call me
the "Sun fox."

The Meerkats

We are meerkats.
You will often see us
standing up,
watching for danger.
Then our families can dig
safely in the sand,
looking for insects to eat.

The Scorpion

I am a scorpion.
You better not run into me!
I have a big stinger
on the tip of my tail.
My sting has strong poison
that hurts
anyone who bothers me.

The Ostrich

I am an ostrich.
I am the biggest bird.
I can run
faster than you ride a bike.
Dancers are jealous
of my fine feathers
and my long legs.

The Camel

I am a camel.
My body stores lots of water
in the hump on my back.
I often carry people
across the hot desert.
I can go a long time
without a drink.

The Dingo

I am a dingo.
Do you think I am a dog?
I am a close cousin
of that pet,
but I am very wild.
I live like a wolf
and hunt animals to eat.

The Horned Devil

I am a horned devil.
My real name is the moloch.
I am a lizard
covered with spikes,
and I change colors
according to my moods.

Please visit our Web site at: www.garethstevens.com
For a free color catalog describing Gareth Stevens Publishing's
list of high-quality books, call 1-800-542-2595 (USA) or
1-800-387-3178 (Canada).

Library of Congress Cataloging-in-Publication Data

Lambilly-Bresson, Elisabeth de.
   [Dans la désert. English]
   Animals in the desert / Elisabeth de Lambilly-Bresson. — North American ed.
      p. cm. — (Animal show and tell)
   ISBN: 978-0-8368-8204-9 (lib. bdg.)
    1. Desert animals—Juvenile literature. I. Title.
QL116.L3413   2007
591.754—dc22   2007002552

This North American edition first published in 2008 by
Gareth Stevens Publishing
A Weekly Reader® Company
1 Reader's Digest Road
Pleasantville, NY 10570-7000 USA

Translation: Gini Holland
Gareth Stevens editor: Gini Holland
Gareth Stevens art direction and design: Tammy West

This edition copyright © 2008 by Gareth Stevens, Inc. Original edition copyright
© 2003 by Mango Jeunesse Press. First published as *Les animinis: Dans le désert*
by Mango Jeunesse Press.

Printed in the United States of America

1 2 3 4 5 6 7 8 9 11 10 09 08 07